JN411722

푸른 비를 맞고

Bathed in Blue Rain

리토피아포에지 · 165
푸른 비를 맞고
인쇄 2025. 8 1 발행 2025. 8. 6
지은이 전재복 역자 최재진Jay Choi·Danielle Scott
펴낸이 정기옥 펴낸곳 리토피아
출판등록 2006. 6. 15. 제2006-12호
주소 21315 인천광역시 부평구 평천로255번길 13, 부평테크노파크M2 903호
전화 032-883-5356 전송032-891-5356
홈페이지 www.litopia21.com 전자우편 litopia999@naver.com

ISBN-978-89-6412-206-8 03810

값 14,000원

전재복 한영시선집

The Collected Poems of Jeon Jae-bok, Korean and English

푸른 비를 맞고

Bathed in Blue Rain

최재진Jay Choi·Danielle Scott 譯

translated by Jay Choi and Danielle Scotts

The Poet's Words

I deemed it but a humble, nameless wildflower. Yet, as it flourished, I discerned it was no mere bloom, but a tender sapling. Incapable of taking even a single step by its own will, it suffered no lack in the art of dreaming.

Through the tender rays of spring, the drenching rains of summer, the whispering gales of autumn, and the solemn hush of winter, the tree wove its dreams, and those dreams burgeoned ceaselessly. Its roots, delving deep and far into the shadowed earth, and its myriad branches, aspiring toward the cerulean heavens, bore at their tips the unfailing procession of spring, summer, autumn, winter—and a fifth, clandestine season, a veritable garden of secrets. These I hold in ardent affection.

Now, as I traverse the seventy-fifth spring of my days, I softly unfurl a dream long veiled. Like sunlight tarrying upon the boughs, like a zephyr tenderly grazing verdant leaves, may the delicate breath of thy presence linger and abide⋯!

Jeon Jae-bok in Okjeong-ri, May 2025.

시인의 말

이름 없는 풀꽃인 줄 알았다.
그러다 자라면서 한 그루 어린나무인 것을 알아차렸을
것이다. 한 발자국도 스스로는 걸어 나갈 수 없었지만,
꿈을 꾸는 데는 부족하지 않았다.

봄 햇살, 여름비, 가을바람, 겨울의 침묵을 견디면서,
나무는 꿈을 꾸고 그 꿈은 자꾸 자랐다. 깜깜한 땅밑으로
멀리멀리 뻗어 나간 뿌리, 푸른 하늘을 향해 내민 수많은
가지 끝에는 어김없이 찾아드는 봄 여름 가을 겨울 그리고
비밀의 화원 같은 다섯 번째 계절이 있었다.
나는 그들을 사랑한다.

그리고 내 생애 일흔다섯 번째 봄을 지나며
조심스레 숨겨둔 꿈 하나 펼쳐 든다.
가지 끝에 머무는 햇살처럼,
초록 잎새 쓰다듬는 바람처럼,
그대의 고운 숨결이 머물다 가기를…!

2025년 5월
옥정리에서 전재복 쓰다

차례

제2부 Summer:Bathed in Blue Rain 여름:푸른 비를 맞고

제3부 Autumn:The Sound of the Landscape 가을:풍경소리

제4부 Winter : Consolation 겨울 : 위로

제5부 The Thirteenth Month : The Scarecrow's Dance
13월 : 허재비의 춤

| 제1부 |

Spring : Bathed in Blue Rain

봄 : 푸른 비를 맞고

Mist · 2

Blowing a magic flute,
the hushed sensuality awakens,
its long tongue flickering,
dancing a sultry sway.

In the flutter of a skirt's hem,
the forest of buildings staggers,
crumbling soft and molten.

Even the river, enduring the endless night,
gasps with heated breath,
shattering silently.

Somewhere between light and shadow,
a world half-crushed, half-tender,
devoured with startling hunger—
only to be spat out,
an anorexia of the soul.

This overflowing, incurable malady—
you, too, suffer its weight.

안개 · 2

마법의 피리를 불며
숨죽인 관능이 일어선다
긴 혀를 날름거리며
간드러진 춤을 춘다

하늘거리는 치맛자락에
빌딩 숲이 비틀거리다
흐물흐물 무너지고

긴 밤을 견뎌온 강물마저
더운 숨을 할딱이며
소리 없이 자지러진다

빛과 어둠의 중간쯤
적당히 뭉개지고
적당히 말랑거리는 세상을
놀라운 식욕으로 먹어치우고는
느닷없이 뱉어내는 거식증

넘쳐서 가실 수 없는 난치병을
너도 앓고 있구나

Where the Flowers Fell

—Cherry Blossoms Fade

Shyly raising their tips,
turning aside to offer leaves,
the blossoms hesitated three days,
then burst open, feigning reluctance.

Rough branches thrust forth flowers first,
a hasty heart laid bare at last—
caught in the act,
and your footsteps turn away so easily,
leaving me to gaze in vain.

With dazzling gestures,
I stole your heart,
returning it as a bed of fallen petals—
Could you know my heart?

꽃 진 자리
—벚꽃 지다

수줍게 촉을 세우고
돌아앉아 잎을 내밀고
꽃이야 한 사흘 뜸을 들이다
못 이긴 척 하나씩 터트려야 했어

거친 가지 불쑥 꽃부터 내밀고선
성급한 마음
끝내 들키고 말았으니
쉽게 돌아서는 그대 발길
하릴없이 바라만 볼 밖에

현란한 몸짓으로
훔친 그대 마음
고운 꽃자리로 돌려드리는
내 마음 그대는 알까 몰라

Spring Breeze

Spoon in hand,
battling the drowsiness pressing my eyelids,
sunlight spills yellow through half-closed eyes—
that's when it begins.

A clandestine stirring,
the prelude to a renaissance—
the dead revive,
beneath frozen earth, crumpled limbs stretch and twitch.

Like a cheer,
leaves and flowers bloom,
a thrill—dream or reality?—
rippling through the world with delight.

Knocking on every shut door,
whispering, *Today' is the day,*
rousing the sleeping soul to exultation—
all because of them,
fanning the flames.

The spring breeze—
their sweet provocation.

봄바람

밥숟가락 든 채
눈꺼풀 눌러 내리는 졸음과 맞서다
스르르 감긴 눈 속으로
햇살이 노랗게 번질 때

그때를 기다렸던 것이다
르네상스의 서막을 준비하는
내밀한 움직임
죽은 것들이 살아나고
언 땅 밑에서도 꼼지락대며
구겨진 팔 다리를 폈다

환호성처럼
잎이 꽃들이 피어나고
꿈인 듯 생시인 듯
기분 좋은 설렘으로 세상은 술렁댔다

닫힌 문마다 두드리며

오늘이 그날이라고
잠자는 내면을 들쑤시고
환호하게 만든 이
자꾸 부채질하는 그들 때문이었다

봄바람, 그들의 선동이 있었던 거다

Germination

Before you opened your heart to me,
I was just a tiny seed cradling dreams,
bound by the limits of a pretty paper packet,
Endless waiting my only world.

What if the soil isn't rich?
A single sturdy grain, carelessly tossed,
taken up without thought, held close—
that's enough.

A hard shell where time stands still,
driven by a blood-red yearning for light,
I'll crash through it—
in a day, two, or three—
with all I am.

Through the sweat-soaked tunnel of darkness, emerging at last, shell shed,
my shy, bare hand reaches out—
how wonderful if it would be the first to hold it
were you.

발아發芽

그대가 가슴을 열어
받아주기 전엔
나는 그냥
꿈을 품은 작은 씨앗이었어
고운 그림 그려진 종이봉투 속이
끝 모를 내 기다림의 한계였지

기름진 땅이 아니면 어때
툭 던져진 옹골찬 작은 알갱이 하나
무심히 받아 들었다가
별 뜻 없이 품었다 해도 괜찮아

시간이 멈춰버린 단단한 껍질
밝음을 향한 핏빛 열망으로
하루 이틀 혹은 사나흘
온몸으로 부딪혀 깨고 말거야

진땀나는 어둠의 터널을 지나
마악 껍질을 벗고 나온
민낯의 수줍은 내손
맨 처음 잡아주는 이
그대였으면 참 좋겠어

Azalea

In the season of wilting blooms,
you brought seeds into the house,
yet stayed silent all along.

When cherry blossoms scattered in chaos,
you spilled your anguish—
a choking flood of crimson.

Mother,
your hidden anguish
was this unbearable.

영산홍

자지러지는 꽃 시절
한집에 시앗을 들이고도
내내 말씀이 없더니

난분분 벚꽃 지자
울컥울컥 쏟아놓은 토혈吐血

어머니
당신의 속앓이가
저토록 아팠네요

Reservoir Scene

Where pine breezes churn the water's ripples,
laughter bursts out like waves.

Sunlight shatters itself,
sprinkling handfuls across the furrows,
relishing the sound as they glitter and stand.

Waterbirds, pecking at newly woken seeds of laughter,
glide over the ridges,
while the thicket, hands behind its back,
tuning its green breath,
quietly unfurls its shadow.

저수지 풍경

솔바람이 갈아엎는 물이랑마다
까르르 일어서는 웃음소리

햇살이 제 몸을 자꾸 조각내어
이랑마다 한 줌씩 뿌려놓고
그것들이 반짝이며 일어서는
소릴 즐긴다

갓 깨어난 웃음 씨앗 쪼아 먹느라
물새 몇 마리
이랑 위로 미끄러지는데

뒷짐 지고 푸른 숨결 고르던 잡목숲이
슬그머니 제 그림자 풀어놓는다

To Longing · 5(Flower of Fate)

In some life,
passing by on an unfamiliar corner,
would we know an unfinished bond?

If, suddenly, I wish to look back,
so be it.

Pausing my steps,
I turn,
and should you glance back unthinking,
let a single flower bloom there.

A longing crossing lifetimes,
quivering like blue starlight—
there,
let one flower bloom.

그리움에게·5(인연 꽃)

어느 생
낯선 길목에서
스쳐 지난들
못다 한 인연 알까마는

불현듯 뒤돌아보고 싶다면
그리하리라

가던 길 멈춰
내가 돌아보고
그대 무심코 돌아볼 때
거기 꽃 한 송이
피었으면 좋겠다

몇 생을 건너온 그리움
푸른 별빛 떨림으로
그곳에
한 송이 꽃
피었으면 좋겠다.

Mother' s Rice Bowl

No trendy barley bibimbap riding wellness waves—
it was a time of desperate hunger,
when even dark barley rice
couldn't dream of a heaping bowl.

The rice that fit the dish,
gulped down with cold water,
sparked a joy that made me hop on tiptoes—
but Mother said, Don't jump, it'll spill.

She sipped water slowly,
her bowl holding just a few grains,
mostly liquid—
my mother's bowl.

Perhaps that's why her stomach
gurgled like flowing water—
grumbling .

어머니의 밥그릇

웰빙바람 타고
폼나게 비벼막는 꽁보리밥이 아녀
참말로 환장하게 배고픈 시절이었느니
시커먼 보리밥도
고봉밥은 엄두를 못 냈어야

그릇 안에 드는 보리밥을
찬물에 뚝뚝 말아먹고
좋아진 기분에 깨금발이라도 뛸라치면
엄니는 밥 꺼진다고 뛰지 말랬어

엄니는 느릿느릿 물을 마셨지
밥알 몇 개 물만 가득한
울엄니의 밥그릇

그래서 엄니의 뱃속에선
물 흐르는 소리가 들렸나벼
꼬르륵~ 꼬르륵

Virgin Fig

Not quite a flower—
can it bear fruit, you wonder?
Show us your bloom, you urge—
but I cannot.

Even the tiniest grass flower
twists with a coy smile,
yet how could I boldly untie my undergarments?

Verdant and boundless,
I trim only my leaves,
passing first blood alone,
binding my budding breasts alone,
nurturing a love half-there, half-not.

When my curves swell beyond hiding,
sweet juices coursing through me,
unbearable at last,
the maiden's gate shyly opens.

Its rosy flesh—
a flower in full bloom,

a love offered with my whole being—
you dare to understand?

童貞女 무화과

꽃도 아닌 것이
열매나 볼 수 있겠나
걱정하시나요
꽃을 내보여라
채근하시나요
그리는 못 하네요

손톱만 한 풀꽃조차
배시시 눈웃음치며
몸을 꼬지만
어떻게 겁 없이 속옷 고름 풀어요

초록으로 무량무량
잎새만 다듬네요
혼자서 초경을 치르고
혼자서 젖멍울 동여매고
있는 듯 없는 듯
속 사랑 키우네요

봉긋봉긋 몸피 불어나고
더는 숨길 수 없을 때
다디단 과즙이 온몸을 돌아
참을 수 없어질 때

수줍게 열리는 처녀의 문

진분홍 속살이
활짝 핀 꽃인 줄
온몸으로 드리는 사랑인 줄
그대, 차마 아시려는지

Mist

Beneath the ice,
I lay still, as if dead,
pressing down my longing
to seep into your veins,
to flow as hot blood.

At dawn, when cunning winds teased too close,
I bit their tongues without mercy,
clinging faintly to a gleaming spear's edge,
screaming this wasn't real—
then woke from the nightmare.

Time unraveled at its own pace,
rumors swirled of someone frozen to death—
whispers gathered into warm tears,
and rain began to fall, a
tender rain melting icy hearts.

The iron bolts of frost gave way,
and I rose, cloaked in intricate freedom,
stretching cramped limbs,
gliding through the gray city,
rousing life with soft kisses.

Oh, and I'll slip into your veins,
flow as pulsing blood,
stirring ripples—
to become flowers, songs,
to become hope.

안개

얼음장 밑에서
죽은 듯 숨죽이고 있었어
당신의 혈관에 스며들어
뜨거운 피로 흐르고 싶은
열망을 누르며

간교하게 집적이는 바람의 혀끝을
사정없이 물어뜯은 새벽엔
번득이는 창끝에 아스라이 매달려서
이건 현실이 아니라고 악을 쓰다
악몽에서 깨어났어

멋대로 풀린 시간은
느린 걸음으로 흘러가고
헐벗은 누군가는 얼어 죽었단
소문이 돌았지
수군거림이 모여 따뜻한 눈물이 되고
비가 내리기 시작했어
언 가슴을 녹이는 따뜻한 비

견고한 얼음 빗장이 풀리고
자유를 촘촘히 입고 날아올랐지
웅크렸던 사지를 풀어

회색도시를 유영하며
부드러운 입맞춤으로 생명을 깨웠어

아, 그리고 당신의 혈관으로 스며들어
뜨거운 피로 흘러갈 거야
두근두근 물살을 일으켜
꽃으로 노래로
희망이 되고 싶어

Brewing Magnolia Flower Tea

You, just twenty, wrapped in downy youth,
a mere glance fills me with joy—
heart fluttering, pacing at a distance.

A spring field thick with barley shoots,
my heart shimmering like heat haze—
unable to hold back,
I reach out.

Azaleas blaze on the hills,
distant doves coo,
pale green races in every direction.

Each plump bud groans with flower-fever,
on this spring day I lay clean rice paper,
welcoming you—
pure magnolia, my bride,
your snowy neck.

To calm your startled heart,
you settle gently,
and I gaze all day,
then with trembling fingertips,

peel back layer after layer.

At the ninth petal's lift—
oh, the secret flower's core.

Only by carving it out,
enduring fervent time,
can we achieve perfect union—
Oh flower, Oh tenderness.

백목련 꽃차를 만들며

갓 스물 솜털 보송한 풋내를 두른 너
바라만 보아도 좋아서
혼자 설레며 두근거리며
먼발치를 서성이다

보리싹 우부룩한 봄 들판
아지랑이 필 것 같은 내 맘
더는 못 참고
못 참고 손을 내민다

진달래 불질하는 산
먼 산 산비둘기 울었던가
사방에선 연초록 줄달음치더라

봉긋한 봉오리마다
꽃 몸살 끙끙 앓는 봄날
정갈한 창호지로 자리 깔고
너를 맞아들인다
순결한 목련, 나의 신부여
희디흰 목덜미여

놀란 가슴 다독이라고
함초롬히 내려앉은 너를

하루쯤 바라만 보다가
떨리는 손끝으로
한 겹 또 한 겹 옷깃을 푼다

아홉 번째 순백의 꽃잎 들춰낸 자리
아, 내밀한 꽃심

그 꽃심 도려내고
뜨거운 시간을 견뎌야만
온전한 합일을 이룬다는
꽃이여 애틋함이여

The Jangdok*

A broad, sturdy frame,
sun-darkened and bare,
its skin prickles under a gentle stroke.

Too heavy to cradle,
unfit for indoors,
I set it in the sunlit yard,
fermenting the jang within.

Silently weathering rain and wind,
embracing sunlight and moonbeams,
its depths ripen.

After seasons of silent discipline,
a profound flavor rises—
rich and resonant.

* A jangdok is a traditional Korean earthenware jar used for fermenting and storing various types of Korean condiments and sauces, such as soy sauce, fermented soybean paste, and red chili paste.

장 독

펑퍼짐한 몸매
검붉게 그을린 민낯
손으로 살살 쓸어보니
소름 돋은 맨살이다

품에 안기도 버거워
방 안에 들일 수 없으니
햇볕 잘 드는 뒤란에
장을 담가 밀쳐 둔다

비바람 말없이 견디고
햇살도 달빛도 품어
깊어진 속내

한세월
묵언수행 끄트머리
웅숭깊은 맛 길어 올린다

| 제2부 |

Summer : Bathed in Blue Rain
여름 : 푸른 비를 맞고

The Pond

A gentle breeze nudges,
tilting its head just a moment— t
hen atop a lotus leaf,
a green frog slips into meditation,
raising a banner of silence, lost in Zen.

Yellow sunlight,
wrapped in fragrance,
a tranquil midday glows.

연못

살풋 밀치는 바람에
감깐 고개만 갸웃하다
이내 명상에 드는 연잎 위
청개구리 한 마리
묵언 패 내걸고 참선에 든다

노란 햇살
향기로 휘감기는
고요한 한낮

The Path to Naesosa Temple*

Parting the lush flesh of July green,
I step into the mountain's crevice.

Like the sturdy calves of a tall scholar,
pine trunks stand in rows, sinews taut,
while from the forest's voluptuous breast,
the breath of life rises, warm and fierce.

A strand of thousand-year wind
brushes by like a dream,
and along a small stream soaking ancient roots,
young wildflowers wash their feet, faces radiant.

A forest of sharing and surrender,
where sunlight settles white on tiled roofs
of an ancient temple—
silently practicing stillness.

*Naesosa Temple (내소사), located at the base of Naebyeongsan Mountain in Jinseo-myeon, Buan County, Jeonbuk State, South Korea, is a historic Korean Buddhist temple established in 633 CE

내소사 가는 길

푸른 칠월의 속살을 헤집고
산의 틈새로 들어선다

훤칠한 장부의 실한 종아리마냥
줄지어 선 전나무 둥치엔 힘줄이 서고
풍만한 초록의 가슴에선
생명의 숨소리 뜨겁다

천년의 바람 한 올
꿈인 듯 스쳐가고
해묵은 뿌리 적시는 작은 물길에
발 씻는 어린 풀꽃들 얼굴이 해맑다

나눔과 순종이 어우러진 숲
고즈넉한 천년고찰 기왓장 위로
햇살 뽀얗게 내려앉아
묵언수행 중이다

When the Seasonal Winds Blow

Between season and season,
wind and wind,
fever sweeps the body,
and a frenzied gallop begins—
a sharpness slicing flesh,
or damp rot thick with mold's scent.

Snapping time's joints,
a radiant era fades,
and the wind crossing seasons arrives—
footsteps familiar yet strange.
Thus, creaking bones
and throbbing head in hand,
I oscillate between hope and despair,
trapped in altitude's grip.

In the ravine of a weary mind,
old coughs pile up with struggle's debris—
always thirst,
ever loneliness.
Perhaps this is the ritual
of shedding one's own skin.

계절풍이 불어올 무렵

계절과 계절 사이
바람과 바람 사이
온몸을 훑는 신열을 깔고
광란의 질주는 시작된다.
살을 저미는 매서움이거나
눅눅한 습기와 곰팡이 냄새거나

툭툭 시간의 마디를 꺾으며
찬란했던 한 시절이 지고 나면
계절을 가로질러 오는 바람
익숙한 듯 낯선 발소리였다
그리하여
삐걱거리는 관절
쑤시는 머리를 싸안고
희망과 좌절을 반복하며
고도에 갇히곤 했다

피폐해진 사고의 골짜기
쿨럭쿨럭 해묵은 기침으로
쌓이는 몸부림의 찌꺼기
늘 목마름이었고
언제나 쓸쓸함이었다.
어쩌면 스스로 껍질을 벗는
의식이기도 했다

Lycoris (Red Spider Lily)

At the wind's crossroads,
a single aching stem
secretly rises.

Tearing my heart apart piece by piece,
I hang red flags
along your passing path,
fainting again and again
in the flare of fevered relapse.

Do you, too, sometimes ache
because of me?
These blooms of blood-tears,
raised in vain—
would you, just once,
cast them a lingering glance?

상사화(꽃무릇)

바람의 길목
남몰래 밀어 올린
아픈 꽃대 하나

가슴살 점점이 뜯어내
그대 지나는 길목
붉은 깃발로 걸어놓고
다시 도지는 열병에
자꾸만 혼절한다
그대도 더러는
나로 하여 아픈지
부질없이 피워 올린
피 울음의 꽃송이를
그대여 한 번은
눈여겨 보시는지

Snail Scholar

Antennae soft and upright,
it reads the heavens' script—

cloudy, then rain.

Decoding the day's weather,
it flattens its body,
slowly, slowly,
surveying the earth's contours.

A fragile, living thing t
oo delicate for hasty judgment,
it pushes life forward
on a precarious thread.

달팽이 書生

곧추세운
무른 더듬이
천문天文을 읽는다

흐리고 비

하루 분량의 날씨를 읽고는
온몸을 깔아
느릿느릿
지리地理를 살핀다

속단하지 못할 살아있음
아슬아슬
생을 밀고 간다

Torrential Rain

I held back for a long time,
swore I'd endure—
days boiling with fever,
wounds from forbidden love festering,
wild mallows blooming boundless
where pus oozed.

A night's lament stacked high
beneath a waning moon,
a single suppressed sob—
touched, it burst like a dam.

You, sprawled atop ash-gray clouds,
weep three days straight
without a mourner's aid.

How many tears
does your unripe body hold?
Flooding streams fill valleys,
blanket fields.

A hidden ache, caught in some knot,
pours out in drumming sobs.

폭우

오래 참았지
무던히 견딘다 했어
신열로 들끓던 몇 날
금지된 사랑에 베인 상처
진물 돋은 자리마다
무량으로 망초 꽃 피더라

달 이울도록 울어쌓던
밤새의 선창先唱으로
오래 견딘 울음 한 꼭지
툭 건드리자
봇물이 터진 게야

암회색 구름을 깔고 퍼질러 앉은 너는
곡비哭婢의 도움 없이도
한 사흘 잘도 운다

여물지 못한 몸 어디에
얼마나 많은 눈물을 품었기에
범람하는 눈물 줄기
골짜기를 메우고 들판을 덮는다

어느 매듭에 걸려 묵힌 속앓이
주룩주룩 소리 내어
울음을 운다

Trumpet Creeper

Don't just leave it in the grass
and pass by—
let a child's reed pipe catch its eye,
nurture a starlike seed or two,
blooming day by day
with bashful, selfless petals.

Plucked for a night's gaze,
set prettily in an icy vase—
even with flower shoes,
it couldn't walk.

A sad legend,
lush with leaves,
folding layers of longing,
hanging red,
tiptoeing over the wall today
in a pitiful dance.

능소화

풀숲에 그냥 두고
지나가시지
초동의 풀피리에 눈 맞추다
별 같은 아이 두엇
씨앗처럼 품어 기르며
날마다 욕심 없이
배시시 꽃 필 텐데

하룻밤 보자시고 우듬지 꺾어
만년 얼음 병에 어여뻐 꽂아두니
꽃신이 있어도
걸을 수 없었네

슬픈 전설
잎새로 무성한 채
그리움 첩첩이 접어
붉게 매달고
오늘도
까치발로 담 밖을 넘보는
애처로운 몸짓

I Envy You, Green Frog

Fretting over swollen currents,
lest your mother's grave wash away,
you wail,
carving her last words into a tombstone.

Don't bury me in the earth—
I loathe the dark pressing my chest.
Spurning even a patch of soil,
she flew off light as air.

Do you roam the mountains
with your wandering son, wind-like?
Missing her, absent even in dreams,
I wield regret's whip too late—
should've defied her,
built a clay home
on a sunny slope.

By the stream,
you, green frog, worrying the rising waters—
I envy you.

청개구리 네가 부럽다

불어난 물살에
어미 묘가 쓸려 갈까
애가 타서 우는 너는
마지막 말씀으로 묘비를 세웠구나

땅속에 가두지 마라
가슴 짓누르는 어둠이 싫다
한 뼘의 땅도 마다하고
당신은 가벼이 날아가시다

바람처럼 떠도는 외아들 따라
산천유람 즐기시는지
꿈에도 안 오시는
당신을 그리며
차라리 말씀을 거역하고
양지바른 산기슭에
흙집 한 평 내드릴 걸
뒤늦은 후회로 회초리를 든다

시냇가
불어나는 물살을 걱정하는
청개구리 네가 부럽다

Ode to Bamboo

Raising its joints,
it claims a room.

Warding off spirits,
it seals each space with care.

Gathering vitality,
girded with resolve—
supple yet unyielding.

Claws thrust deep into the earth,
blue veins pulse on its feet—
a steadfast backbone,
its fingers pierce the sky.

From wherever it came,
how could one not rejoice?

A prop for the sun,
a rod to fish time,
a flute stealing a sliver of the heart.

대나무 찬讚

마디를 치고
방 한 칸을 들인다

귀신도 넘보지 못하게
칸칸이 결계를 친다

끌어모은 정기
뱃심으로 두르고
유연하나
꺾이지 않는 결연함

땅 밑으로 욱여넣은 발톱
발등엔 푸른 힘줄 선명하다
든든한 뒷심으로
천공을 찌르는
저 손가락질

어디서 무엇이 된들
기쁘지 않으랴

해를 떠받치는 바지랑대
세월을 낚는 낚싯대
마음 한 점 훔치는 저 퉁소 소리

Bamboo Shoots

A thriving bamboo grove,
leaning on robust youth.

Fearless, soaring pride—
how fiercely must it train
to stand so upright?
How deep must it grow
to be empty yet full to the brim?

Threats and coaxing
endured like death underground—
don't presume to know
and call it shoots overnight.
These are towers of patience,
stacked layer by layer,
chewing bitter weeds.

우후죽순

울울창창 왕대나무숲
탄탄한 젊음에 기댄다

거침없이 치솟은 당당함
얼마나 호되게 단련하면
저토록 올곧을 수 있는지
얼마나 깊어지면
비우고도 가득 찰 수 있는지

으름장도 회유도
죽은 듯 견뎌낸 땅밑 시간
허투루 넘겨짚고
하루아침 우후죽순이라
아는 체 말라
독풀을 씹어 삼킨 인고의 돌탑이
켜켜이 쌓인 것을

Patching Up Hunger

A thirst dragged
from some distant life, perhaps—
from my first breath,
I craved love by instinct.

A hunger life could never sate,
a shadow-thirst trailing close.

Not with matter—
how then to fill it?
I ground my bones,
but hope was a cracked gourd,
neither holding nor soaking through.

Just once,
I longed for a love
that needed me alone—
but that desire, castrated,
left kneeling knees
festering with sores.

In the cold wind,
mending hunger,
tear-flowers shine bright.

허기를 깁다

어느 먼 생에서
끌고 온 갈증이었을까
첫 숨을 뱉는 순간
본능으로 사랑이 고팠다

한 번도 충족하게
채울 수 없던 삶의 허기
그림자처럼 따라붙는 목마름

물질이 아닌
무엇으로 채우리라
뼈를 갈았으나
바램은 늘 실금 간 조롱박
고일 수도 적실 수도 없었다

단 한 번만이라도
나 아니면 안 되는
사랑을 갈구했으나
그건 거세당한 욕망
꿇린 무릎은
덧난 상처로 질척이고

시린 바람 속
허기를 깁는
눈물 꽃이 환하다

Bathed in Blue Rain

Bathed in blue rain,
If I bore a child—

Lips blackened under scorching sun,
a heart splitting wide—
stepped rough, thunder-roaring blue rain comes.
Shamelessly rolling,
I'd birth a blue child.

With loud retching morning sickness,
I want to bear a child
that never wilts.

푸른 비를 맞고

푸른 비를 맞고
아이 하나 낳았으면

땡볕에 입술 까맣게 타다가
쩍쩍 갈라지는 가슴패기
거칠게 밟고
우레로 오시는 靑雨
부끄러움도 잊은 양
온몸 던져 뒹굴며
푸른 아이 하나 배고 싶다

헛구역질 입덧도 요란하게
시들지 않는
아이 하나 낳고 싶다

Not You, But Me

How far must I go
to cool this heat?
Trapped in thoughts of you,
unrelenting,
fever boils within.

Over the hill outside the village,
around the bend,
hiding even my shadow—
would that do it?
Run or stop, you cling.

My insides, now full of you—
not you, but me—
where must I go to find myself?

너 말고 나

얼마큼 멀어지면
식어질까
한시도 떠나지 않는
생각에 갇혀
펄펄 열이 끓어

동구 밖 고갯마루
꼴딱 넘어가면
길모퉁이 돌아서
그림자마저 감추면
그러면 될까?
달려도 멈춰도 따라붙는 너

어느새 너 하나로 가득 찬 내 안
너 말고 나
어디로 가면 찾을까

| 제3부 |

Autumn : The Sound of the Landscape
가을 : 풍경소리

Okjeong-ri Diary(Autumn)

A shiver runs through
the sunflower's pockmarked face,
a basket of sunlight spilling down in a rustle.
Holding up its full-term belly,
the sunflower twists its body with effort.

A red-tailed dragonfly
sets the autumn field ablaze.
Even the sunlight tumbling in grains
is hastily gobbled up,
and the fruit, cheeks plump, falls into a deep sleep.

In blue smoke,
green soybeans pop and shed their skins.

옥정리 일기(가을)

오소소 소름 돋은
해바라기 버짐 핀 얼굴 위
차르르 쏟아지는 햇살 한 소쿠리
만삭의 배를 떠받들고
해바라기 힘겹게 몸을 뒤챈다

고추잠자리 붉은 꼬리로
불 지핀 가을 밭
낟알로 뒹구는 햇살마저
서둘러 주워 먹고는
탱탱한 볼로 단잠에 든 열매

푸른 연기 속
풋콩이 톡톡 옷을 벗는다

The Sound of Wind Chimes

At the eaves of the grand templel,
a single fish
comes alive
with the slightest thread of wind.

Clang, clang, clang—
a fish swimming against the breeze.

A reckless fish, spurning water,
lives a thousand years
by the wind's sermon.

풍경소리

대웅전 처마 끝
물고기 한 마리
바람 한 올에도
살아나고 있었다

땡그랑 땡그랑 ~
바람을 거슬러 헤엄치는 물고기

물을 거부한 발칙한 물고기가
바람의 법문으로
천년을 사는구나

Around the Time of Cheoseo*

An unguarded window flung wide—
a thread of dawn's chill barges in,
caught in a dry throat
with a cough.

The sticky clinging,
the long sleepless hours,
hide in the red shade of the crape myrtle blossoms.
With the sound of a summer cold's cough,
leaves fall in a sudden shower.

The midday heat, boiling with noise,
the shrieks and clamor of a whole season—
who knows if the trees' ears remain unscathed?

When the roar that threatened to burst eardrums,
wandering through time and space,
shifts from the air to settle beneath the doorstep,
the fierce resistance of the past season,
as hot as the heatwave,
is sealed in the jar of self-restraint.

*Cheoseo, meaning "End of Heat," is one of the 24 solar terms in the traditional Korean lunar calendar, typically falling around August 22 - 24 in the Gregorian calendar.

처서 무렵*

무방비로 열어둔 창문
불쑥 새벽 냉기를 물고
바람 한 올 넘어오다
콜록
마른 목구멍에 걸린다

치근대던 끈적임
오랜 불면을 앓아온 시간이
배롱나무 붉은 꽃그늘로 숨어들고
여름감기 바튼 기침소리로
낙엽이 후두둑 진다

소리로 들끓던 한낮의 폭염
한 계절 내내 몰아치던
비명과 아우성에
나무들 귓구멍은 탈 없는지 몰라

고막이 터져버릴 듯
시공간을 떠돌던 함성이
공중에서 섬돌 밑으로
자리를 옮겨 앉을 때쯤
폭염만큼이나 뜨거웠던
지난 계절 내 거친 저항도

자숙自肅의 항아리에 봉인한다

*처서는 '더위가 끝나는 날'을 뜻하며, 한국의 전통 음력 24절기 중 하나로, 일반적으로 양력 8월 22일에서 24일경에 해당합니다.

The withering of the Wood-Water Chrysanthemum

A lifetime of noble poverty
bore only barren flowers, no pistils.
With an empty chest,
I couldn't dream of sticky gazes—
how freshly tearful it feels now.

To call the soul crossing into the next world,
I fling a plain muslin robe over the roof—
alas, too late!
It's a tomb of layered white blooms.

Piling up white flowers
like a generous burial mound,
I search for worthy seeds,
but all are hollow—
no pistil holds a single one.

The unbearable lightness of being—
in a whistling breeze,
it lifts entirely away,
that flower tomb.

목수국木水菊 지다

평생을 끌고 온 청빈淸貧이
암술도 못 갖춘 헛꽃만 피웠다
빈 가슴으로야
꿈에도 못 품어 본 끈끈한 눈길
새삼 눈물겨워라

이승을 넘어가는 혼백을 부르려
무명 홑적삼 지붕 위로 던지는데
아뿔사, 너무 늦었구나!
겹겹이 하얀 꽃 무덤이다

덩실한 봉분 같은
흰 꽃들을 부려놓고
쓸만한 종자種子를 찾아보나
모두가 헛헛하다
씨를 품은 암술은 어디에도 없다

참을 수 없는 존재의 가벼움
소슬바람에
통째로 날아간다.
저 꽃 무덤

Late Autumn, Around Three in the Afternoon

Late autumn, three o'clock—
without wind, leaves fall in a rush.
Just nudge them,
and they'd weep without excuse.

On the weathered wall,
sunlight lingers like a favor,
but the warmth slipped away long ago.

At the tips of branches, drained of sap,
a few leaves still cling,
unable to let go—
their rims red as tearful eyes.

늦가을 오후 세 시쯤

늦가을 오후 세 시쯤
바람 없이도 후두둑
낙엽 진다
건들기만 해봐라
핑계 없어 못 우는데

낡은 담벼락엔
선심인 듯 햇살이 머물지만
진즉 빠져나간 온기
물기 걷어간 나뭇가지 끝에서

차마 손 놓지 못한
잎사귀 몇 장
눈자위가 붉다

The Yoke

It'll lighten—
this suffocating yoke of habit,
if I cast it off entirely.

Who'd complain
if I wore shoes on my head with flair
and a hat on my feet?

For a day, I'll stand bare
under the sun.

From my crown, branches will sprout,
green leaves budding thick
on all ten fingers.

From toes, trapped and glum in shoes,
tiny roots will wriggle free.

Rooted in the earth,
gulping sweet water,
a drowsy sleep might come—
or dreams I'd lost.

Too clear to be seen,
a hollow-chested tree
might meet me there.

굴레

가벼워질 거야
숨 막히는 관습慣習의 굴레
훌훌 벗어 버리면

신발을 멋스럽게 머리에 쓰고
모자를 발에 신는다고
누가 뭐라겠어?

하루쯤은 벌거벗고
햇살 아래 서 있을 테야

정수리에선 쑥쑥 가지가 자라고
열 손가락 가득
초록 잎새 돋아날 거야
신발에 갇혀서

노상 우울하던 발가락에선
꼬물꼬물 잔뿌리도 자라나겠지

땅속에 뿌리를 박고
단물에 꿀꺽꿀꺽 목을 축이면
노곤한 잠이 올지도 몰라
잃어버린 꿈을 꿀 지도 몰라

너무 맑아서
아무에게도 보이지 않는
가슴이 텅 빈 나무 하나
만날지 몰라

Flowing By

—Wind Blows, Rain Falls

When the wind blows,
every joint of my limbs opens—
I become a wooden wind instrument.
Following the wind's tune,
a low whisper —
sometimes a tremor,
sometimes an endless echo.

When rain falls,
wherever drops touch,
a current forms—
down to the fine veins of fingertips and toes,
murmuring low, pooling into streams.
Past the empty yard,
it softly soaks the dry grass.

A cold shadow
stares at me, unmoving—
then transparent sunlight reaches out,
gently patting
tear-brimmed shoulders,
a furrowed chest,
stroking again and again.

흘러가다

—바람 불고 비

바람이 불면
사지삭신 마디마디가 열려
나는 한 개 목관악기가 되려하네
바람의 소리를 따라
우우우~
깊은 여운으로 길을 열지
때로는 떨림으로
가끔은 끝없는 울림으로

비가 내리면
빗방울 닿는 자리마다
흐름이 되어
손발톱 끝 실핏줄까지
나직나직 소리 내어
여울지려네
공허한 뜰을 지나
마른 풀숲까지 자분자분 적시겠네

시린 그림자
우두커니 바라보는 날
투명한 햇살이 손을 뻗어와
눈물 그렁한 어깨를
고랑 지는 가슴을
가만가만 다독이겠네
자꾸 쓰다듬겠네

Fallen Leaves, A Dance of Parting

I know—
bearing frost at dawn,
the waning moon crosses the long night,
feigning indifference
with hollow coughs,
holding back rising sobs.

I know—
it must leap
into the thousand-foot abyss.
The tender gesture of carving out love—
even the sunlight watches, hushed.

Now, let go of my hand.
I'll leap—
accept this radiant dance of farewell.
I'll carry your love with me.

낙엽, 別離의 춤

알아요
신새벽 무서리 이고
그믐달 저렇게
긴 밤을 건너와서는
짐짓 아무렇지 않은 듯
헛기침만 하지만
차오르는 울음 참고 있다는 걸

알아요
천 길 낭떠러지
뛰어내려야 한다는 걸
사랑을 도려내는 일
그 아린 몸짓
햇살도 숨죽여
지켜보고 있다는 걸

이제 잡은 손 놓으세요
뛰어내릴게요
찬란한 별리別離의 춤사위
받아주세요
그대 사랑 안고 갈게요

The Tree' s Fingerprint

A careless sweep
drives out late autumn.

In mournful parting,
eyes red from days of weeping,
a face yellowed by chronic wheezing,
even the reckless green bravado leaping down—
the tree's languid fingerprints
gather in one place,
rustling, each flaunting its shining record.
Still, it's beautiful.

Who hasn't had a radiant season?

Nodding to each weary life,
making room in tight spaces,
we'll stroke each other's bent backs.

When the time we've embraced
turns worn fingerprints to fertile soil,
will a sweet fragrance rise from our bodies—

like liquor ripening
in a mottled clay jar?

나무의 지문指紋

무심한 비질에
저문 가을이 내몰린다

설운 이별에
몇 날을 울어 붉은 눈자위,
태생적 천식
쌕쌕대는 기침으로
누렇게 뜬 얼굴,
겁 없이 뛰어내려
건들대는 초록의 허세까지
유장한 나무의 지문들이
한곳에 모였다
저마다 빛나는 이력을 들이대며
부시럭거린다
그래도 아직은 아름답구나

누군들 빛나는 시절이 없었을까

각각의 고단한 생애
고개 끄덕이고
좁은 자리 더 당겨
곁을 내줄 즈음
우리도 서로

굽은 등을 쓰다듬겠지

끌어안은 시간을 버무려
헤진 지문이 거름으로 승화될 때
온몸에선 달큰한 향기가 날까?
뽀골뽀골 옹기항아리에
술 익는 냄새 같은

Hunger

"Where's my food?"
The old mother, well-fed three times a day,
who served generous portions,
hears her son's familiar voice
and first says, "I'm hungry,
I haven't eaten."

The mother who worried over her son's meals
is absent now,
tracing the far backroads of life.

Bones that bore ninety-some years strike
too weary for the body's weight—
yet in an empty stomach,
something unfilled
still hungers.

허기

왜 밥 안 줘?
세끼 잘 드시고
푸짐하게 내놓으셨다는 노모는
낯익은 아들의 목소리에
제일 먼저 배고프다 이른다
밥 안 먹었다고

아들의 밥을 걱정하던
어머니는 지금 부재중
먼 먼 생의 뒤안길을
더듬고 계시다

구십몇 해를 지탱한 뼈마디는
육신의 무게가 버거워
파업 중인데
속없는 밥통
채우지 못한 무엇이
아직도 고픈가 보다

Dry Tree

A dry tree,
seated in a wheelchair—
only twigs remain, brittle, crumbling
in the slightest breeze.

Sparse white hair
on frail shoulders, heavy with time's dust,
shaking endlessly—
"No, no,"
"Yes, yes," again and again.

What's it pushing away?
Hands on the armrests
keep brushing something off.

Shoo, shoo—
shaking off
a lifetime gone by.

마른나무

마른나무 한 그루
휠체어에 앉으셨다
삭정이만 남아
건들바람에도
바슬바슬 부서지겠다

세월의 더께가 버거운
가녀린 어깨 위 성근 백발
간단없이
아니, 아니라고
그래, 그렇다고
자꾸 흔든다

무얼 내치려는지
팔걸이에 올린 손
그마저 자꾸 털고 계시다

훠이훠이
지나온 한 생을
털어내고 계시다

Unjust Powerlessness

A cherry tree,
ailing for years,
half-rotted—
its bark peels at a touch.

Yet it persists—
along a spine half-broken,
it drags news from the earth below.
Soon, through sweat-soaked vessels
climbed thousands of times,
it'll light a string of blossoms—
like last year, the year before,
flowers bright with aching sadness.

Pressing an ear to the dark hollow,
deep inside, someone
seems to dig a cave—
in tomb-like silence,
a faint scratch, scratch,
an illusion of water breaking through.

In some damp crevice,
larvae gnaw at living wood—

the old caterpillar's ravenous hunger
hides there too.
A sudden sting in my heart,
a creeping itch through my body.

This fear, this unjust helplessness—
as if it might all be devoured
in an instant.

억울한 무기력

몇 년에 걸쳐 시름시름 앓던
벚나무 하나
반쪽은 이미 삭아서
손끝으로도 뜯겨 나간다

그런데도 참 용하다
반도 채 못남은 등뼈를 타고
땅 밑 소식을 한사코 퍼올린다
머잖아 수천 번 오르내리느라
땀 젖은 물관을 따라
줄줄이 꽃불도 밝힐 게다
작년처럼 재작년처럼
슬프도록 환한 꽃불

가만히 깜깜한 구멍에 귀를 들이대니
저 안 깊숙이 누가
동굴 하나 파고 있나 보다
무덤 같은 적막 속에
사부작 사부작
물길 트는 소리 환청으로 듣는데

거기 어느 음습한 틈새
살아있는 나무의 살점을

먹어치우는 애벌레
늙은 송충이의 왕성한 식욕도
숨어있는갑다
갑자기 심장이 따끔거린다
온몸이 근질거린다

어느 순간 몽땅 먹혀버릴 것 같은
두렵고 억울한 이 무기력

| 제4부 |

Winter : Consolation
겨울 : 위로

Draft Stopper Paper*

On a stiff hemp towel,
starched to the brim,
after summer has rubbed away,
a fistful of light
plunges through the bright breath of window paper.

Beyond still, outstretched hands,
a breeze flows—
a single flame flickering alive,
blushing cheeks,
whispering secrets into my ear.

*Draft stopper paper is munjangji, also known as Korean traditional window paper or hanji when used specifically for windows, is a type of handmade paper crafted from the inner bark of the mulberry tree.

문풍지

풀 센 베수건에
여름이 묻어간 뒤
창호지 환한 숨결 밑으로
곤두박질쳐 내달아 오는
빛 한 움큼

가만히 손 벌린 등 너머
호르르
불붙는 바람 한 개피
볼 붉혀 귓속말을
매달고 있다

Reset

If someone asked me
to erase all the time gone by
and start anew,
I'd return to twenty, perhaps—
that twenty I left behind, so bland,
I'd rewrite it bold and vivid.

I'd plunge into saltwater,
sneeze in spicy red pepper,
and some days meet cotton candy.
If I could, I'd take the winding backroads,
not the straight path,
and speak to the things I missed.

To the small things I rushed past,
eyes fixed ahead,
I'd stamp my gaze on each one,
praise them as they are.
I'd love loud and reckless,
staking my life on it—
most of all, I'd learn what I liked,
what I was good at.

After writing twenty so richly,
I'd leap back to sixty or so—
having soothed the sweet, sour, bitter, spicy, salty,
I could turn to myself
with a little calm,
and that sixty feels just right.

리셋

지나온 시간을 모두 지우고
다시 시작하겠느냐
누가 내게 묻는다면
스물 즈음으로 돌아갈까 해
두고 온 스물이 너무 밍밍해서
돌아가 다시 진하게 써 볼 테야

소금물에 푹 잠겨도 보고
매운 고춧가루에 재채기도 해보고
솜사탕을 만나는 날도 있겠지
가능하면 쭉 뻗은 길보다는
구불구불 샛길을 걸으며
놓쳐버린 것들에게 말을 붙여봐야지

앞만 보느라
지나쳐버린 사소한 것들에
모두 눈도장 찍어주며
있는 그대로 칭찬도 해줘야지
목숨 걸고 떠들썩하게 사랑도 해볼 거야
무엇보다도 내가 무얼 좋아했는지
무엇을 잘할 수 있었는지 알아볼 테야

그렇게 진하게 스물을 써 보고

나는 훌쩍 예순 즈음으로 돌아오고 싶어
달고 시고 쓰고 맵고 짠맛
모두 다독거려놓고
조금은 담담하게 내게로 돌아설 수 있는
예순 즈음이 참 좋거든

Winter Bud

All alone,
I endure—
a needle's piercing chill
tearing to my bones,
lips clenched tight
lest a groan escapes.

Flesh bitten
by layered fangs,
sap flows out—
toward you,
I take a step.

To bloom a radiant spring,
I pour
every ounce of strength.

겨울눈(아린芽鱗)

오롯이
혼자 견디는 중이다
뼛속까지 헤집는
극한의 바늘 끝
행여 신음 소리 새나갈까
앙다문 입술

겹겹이 세운 송곳니로
깨물린 살점
진액으로 흘러
그대 향해 한 발짝
내딛는 중이다

찬란한 봄을 피우려
혼신의 힘을
쏟아붓는 중이다

Last Will

It's not about the money.
When consciousness leaves me,
don't take me to a hospital.
No rash cuts with a knife,
no stripping me bare,
strung up with tubes
for a spectacle—
preserve the last dignity of a human.

Remember I hate noise and clutter.
Don't tie me to a hospital
for a money feast.
Just let me rest in the nature I love—
let me smell the wind,
hear the trees,
let warm sunlight and blue starlight
stand guard over me.

Don't let me linger
as a tiresome memory.
Just for a moment,
let me feel your warm touch nearby.
〉

Don't I feel the cold so keenly?
Especially my knees—
cover them warmly.

It's not about the money.
When consciousness slips away,
don't struggle to hold me back.
Just let me linger in your eyes a little longer.

유언

돈 아까워 그러는 게 아니다
의식이 나를 떠나거든
병원에 데려가지 말아다오
섣불리 칼을 대지도 마라
발가벗겨 놓고
주렁주렁 줄에 매달려
구경거리 되지 않게 해라
인간의 마지막 존엄은 지켜다오

시끄럽고 복잡한 건
딱 질색인 걸 기억해다오
병원에 묶어놓고
돈 잔치 하지마라
그저 내 좋아하는 자연 속에
나를 머물게 해다오
바람의 냄새를 맡게 하고
나무들의 소리를 듣게 해라
따뜻한 햇볕 푸른 별빛이
나를 지키게 해다오

지긋지긋한 기억으로
오래 있지 않게 해다오
잠시만 가까이에서

따뜻한 체온을 느끼게 해 주렴

나는 유독 추위를 타지 않니?
특히 무릎이 시리지 않도록
따뜻하게 덮어다오

돈 아까워 그러는 게 아니다
의식이 나를 떠나거든
어찌해보려 애쓰지 마라
잠시만 너희 눈 안에 머물게 해다오

Frost Flower Letter

I never craved color,
so there's nothing to fade—
though green I might have dared to hold,
who'd say I longed
to be dyed by red flowers or yellow leaves?

On a night when cold seeps to my bones,
beneath blue starlight,
I stretch trembling hands
to write a long, long letter.

Just once, just once,
I want my love to blaze hot,
like that blood-drenched flower,
like dazzling yellow leaves too bright to bear.

Tearing my frozen heart bit by bit,
kneeling on icy ground,
I write with numb hands—
before your touch can reach,
before you trace a single line,
it melts into cold droplets.
Have you read my frost flower's burning letter?

서리꽃 편지

색깔을 탐하지 않았으니
빛바랠 일도 없겠지요만
초록이야 감히 마음에 품었을까마는
붉은 꽃엔들 노란 잎엔들
물들고픈 마음 없을라구요

뼛속까지 한기寒氣가 스미는 밤
푸른 별빛 아래 곱은 손을 뻗어
길고 긴 편지를 씁니다

한 번만 꼭 한 번만
내 사랑도 뜨겁게 피워내고 싶어요
선혈 낭자한 저 꽃처럼
눈부셔 차마 못 볼 샛노란 잎새처럼

얼어붙은 심장 점점이 뜯어내어
언 땅에 무릎 꿇고
시린 손으로 써 내려간 편지
그대 손길 닿기도 전에
한 줄 미처 짚어가기도 전에
온기 없는 물방울로 스러지고 말
서리꽃 뜨거운 편지 읽어보셨나요

In December

I should've savored it, melted it slow—
even with a full pocket itching to spend,
I shouldn't have been so reckless.

Three hundred sixty-something candies,
puffed up with empty air—
I crunched them, grumbled at their sameness,
rolled them around,
tossed them anywhere.
I shouldn't have been so careless.

A loosened pocket,
a few rattling coins—
nothing to buy
before December's clear window.

Counting the clinks in my pocket
for days,
I swallow dry,
fold up this futile time
in a hurry.

12월에

아끼며 녹여 먹을걸 그랬지
주머니가 두둑해서 좀이 쑤셔도
함부로 그러는게 아니었어

삼백예순 몇 개의 알사탕에
헛바람 가득해져서
아작아작 깨물어도 보고
매양 한 맛이라 타박도 하고
이리 저리 굴리다
아무 데나 처박기도 했어
함부로 그러는 게 아니었는데

헐거워진 주머니
딸랑거리는 몇 개의 동전으론
아무것도 살 수 없는
12월의 투명한 창 앞

주머니 속 딸각대는
몇 날을 확인하곤
마른 침만 꼴깍 삼키다
서둘러
허망의 시간을 접는다

Winter Rose

No way, it can't be—
a few days of spring-like sun
on dry gravel and frozen earth—
that's not spring.
A thread of water
in the ice's crack—
that's not spring.

No way, it can't be—
when a thought brushes somewhere,
my stone heart thumps wild,
giggling foolishly—
surely something's gone wrong,
but no way, it can't be—
this tender thing, love?

A winter rose blooming out of season,
even if it freezes into ice flowers,
I can't blame you
for teasing me with spring—
it's my fault for blushing so weakly.

Even if I fade into a shard of ice,
thank you, dear—
for a moment, I was a flower.

겨울 장미

설마 그럴 리가요
메마른 자갈밭 꽁꽁 언 땅에
사나흘 봄날 같은 햇살이 비쳤다고
봄일 리가요
얼음장 틈새
실낱같은 물길이 생겼다고
봄일 리가요

설마 그럴 리가요
어딘가에 생각이 닿으면
바윗돌 심장이 제멋대로 콩닥대고
일없이 실실거리는 게
큰 탈이 붙은 건 맞는데요
설마 그럴 리가요
그것이 야들야들 사랑일 리가요

철없이 핀 겨울 장미
선 채로 얼음꽃이 된다 한들
봄인 양 장난을 걸어온
그대를 탓하다니요
맥없이 얼굴 붉힌 내 탓인걸요

한 조각 얼음으로 스러진다 해도
고마워요 그대,
한순간 꽃이었네요

Consolation

With no eyes in the back of my head,
I can't see the sadness
hiding behind a smiling face.

If only I could see behind me
without turning,
I'd call out the trembling weakness
lurking beneath bravado,
pat it gently—
"It's okay, it's okay."

Like wiping off makeup,
at the hour of folding the day,
shedding the heavy shells
piled on thick,
I finally stretch my weary limbs.

Living is
layering armor each day,
polishing shields,
sharpening arrowheads,
aiming at someone's chest,
and taking wounds from arrows returned.

If I could stretch my arms twice as long,
I'd wrap them quietly around my back,
stroking my lonely, tired spine
like a mother,
endlessly,
until the sorrow melts away.

위로

뒤 꼭지에 눈이 없어서
웃는 얼굴 뒤에 숨은
슬픔을 보지 못한다

고개 돌리지 않아도
뒤를 볼 수만 있다면
허세 뒤에 숨어
벌벌 떠는 나약함을 불러내어
괜찮다 괜찮다 토닥여 줄 텐데

화장을 지우듯
하루를 접는 시간
두덕두덕 걸쳐 입은
무거운 껍질을 벗으며
비로소 힘들었을 四肢를 편다

살아간다는 것은
날마다 갑옷을 포개 입는 일
방패를 닦고
화살촉을 가는 일
누군가의 가슴을 향해
활시위를 당기고
되돌아온 화살에 상처를 입는 일

〉

팔을 두 배쯤 늘릴 수만 있다면
가만히 등 뒤로 두 팔을 돌려
어머니가 했던 것처럼
하염없이
쓸쓸하고 지친 등을 쓰다듬어주리
설움이 녹을 때까지 쓰다듬어 주리

Island Keeper

I steeled my heart
and bought an island—
the chaotic world grew too heavy.

Locking the door to the outside,
in a low-walled yard,
I hung a single splendid scene.

Waking the light alone,
quenching the light alone,
I'd be the island's keeper, I said—

yet my unshrinking ears
itch endlessly,
and blind feelers
still tiptoe
toward the door.

섬지기

맘 다져먹고
섬 하나 샀다
어지러운 세상이 버거워서

세상 밖으로 난 문을 닫아걸고
나지막한 울안에
수려한 풍경 하나 내걸었다

홀로 빛을 깨우고
홀로 빛을 사르고
섬지기나 되겠다 했다

그래놓고도
퇴화 되지 못한 귀는
노상 가렵고
눈 먼 더듬이는
아직도 문밖으로
까치발을 세운다

A Lost Key

Let's not strain—
you, standing
as an unclimbable wall.

Before a padlock bolted shut,
why recall
a silver key,
drowned faint in galaxy waters?

The spool of time, unwound,
is flung into thorns—
on a tangled body,
barbs sprout wild.

No need to ache and collapse
from foolish hope again—
a lost key,
sinking heavy, rusting away.

잃어버린 열쇠

애쓰지 말자
넘지 못할
벽으로 서 있는 너

굳게 틀어 쥔 자물통 앞에서
기억도 아득하게
은하 물에 빠뜨린 은빛 열쇠를
떠올리다니

풀려버린 시간의 얼레는
덤불에 던져지고
얼기설기 엉킨 몸에
가시는 웃자라는데

가당찮은 기대 때문에
또 무너져 아프지 말자
무겁게 가라앉아 녹슬어갈
잃어버린 열쇠

Making Kimchi

A tight-furled cabbage,
split clean in half—
a season ripened yellow,
packed full and firm.

Sprinkle coarse salt,
press it into brine,
tame its sharp edge.

The swagger that rose
through harsh seasons,
the anger,
the rough corners that scarred each other—
press them down into saltwater,
let them wail for half a day.

In clear water,
rinse off lingering grit,
shake off petty pride—
then, yielding,
mix into vibrant, welcoming spice.

A sack of love,

a few tubs of back-bending sighs—
toss them together,
let it ripen deliciously.

김치를 담그며

속이 꽉 찬 가슴배기
반으로 쩍 가른다
옹골차게 들어차
노랗게 여문 한계절

왕소금 설설 뿌려
소금물에 눌러 넣고
날 선 기를 다스린다

호된 계절을 건너며
무시로 일어서던 우쭐거림
혹은 노여움
서로를 상처 내던 거친 모서리
꾹꾹 눌러 소금물에 담가두고
한나절쯤 목 놓아 울게 하다

맑은 물에
남은 티끌 씻어내고
알량한 자존심도 털어내고
살갑게 품 펼치는
맛깔스런 양념에
못 이긴 척 몸을 섞는다
〉

사랑 한 포대
허리 휘는 한숨 몇 동이
썩썩 버무려
맛나게 익어가라

Frostbite Flower(Adonis)

All I can offer, with nothing to give,
 is to fling my body
onto frozen earth,
to wound myself—
with bare feet and wet blood,
to melt the ice.

With warm blood, drop by drop,
I thaw the ground beneath,
blooming vivid yellow
 like the sun.

To you,
who first wiped my tears
and called my name,
I bring spring's first news.

얼음새꽃(복수초)

가진 것 없는 내가
할 수 있는 일이란
언 땅에 온몸 던져
상처를 내는 일
맨발에 젖은 핏물로
얼음을 녹이는 일

방울방울 솟는 더운 피로
발밑을 녹여
해를 닮은 샛노랑
환하게 피워낸다

가장 먼저
눈물 닦아 이름 불러준
그대에게

| 제5부 |

The Thirteenth Month : The Scarecrow's Dance
13월 : 허재비의 춤

A Bird Filling with Wind

Emptying my bones,
I fill them with wind.

Most days lived—
poverty and hunger,
the feather-light weight
of endless solitude.
In a storehouse emptied to fullness,
the wind of silence
cracks its whip.

I always dreamed of flight—
soaring long through the sky.

To lighten further,
I hollow my marrow,
endure the hunger,
fill myself
with wind nursed by loneliness.

바람을 채우는 새

뼈마디를 비우고
바람을 채운다

살아온 날
대부분은 빈곤과 허기
늘 고독했던 날들의
깃털 같은 무게
비워서 충만한 곳간엔
침묵의 바람이
채찍을 휘둘렀다

늘 비상을 꿈꿨다
오래오래 창공을 나는

더 가벼워지기 위해
뼛속을 비운다
허기를 견디고
고독이 키운 바람을
가득 채운다

A Drowning Island

When my heart tears to shreds,
rising in silent screams,
I go to the sea in my mind.
The weight I've swallowed
crushes my shoe tips—
I stare down, throat aching.

Water wets my ankles,
submerges calves, navel—
waves slap my chest.
A flicker of sorrow floats like seaweed.

Water fills my eyes,
hair weeps loose like a flag.

A lone island
sinks slowly underwater—
so quiet,
no one notices its drowning.

An island everywhere,
an island nowhere—
one island, one me.

익사하는 섬

마음이 너덜너덜 찢어져
소리 없이 아우성으로 뜨는 날
생각 속 바다로 간다
안으로 눌러 삼킨 무게 때문에
짓이겨진 신발 코
목 아프게 내려다본다

발목이 젖고
종아리와 배꼽이 잠기고
가슴으로 물살이 친다
얼핏 검불 같은 설움이 뜬다

눈으로 물이 차오르고
깃발처럼 풀어져 흐느끼는 머리카락

고독한 섬 하나
물 밑으로 천천히 가라앉는다
너무 고요해서
아무도 섬의 익사溺死를
알아채지 못한다

어디에나 있고
어디에도 없는
섬 하나, 나 하나

A Staggering Sea

Is it the left head's ache or the right that tilts my steps aside? The moonlight boiled all night, steam rising in vain effort—I knew it was wasted strength. My falling head's weight needs a hot air balloon. My soul's still plant-born, yet forced to eat rank animal flesh. I stroke my swelling body with mournful eyes. When the bloated belly's too much, or nausea overwhelms, I hug the toilet upside-down, retch—half-melted animal bones, one-eyed stares, half-hearts pulsing, spilling out—and mountains of recyclable plastic vomited too. My soul's still plant! Plant! Plant!—I chant. Only when I touch the ribs choking under fat, nearly snapped, do I know this body's still mine. Oh, those throbbing, bruised ribs—what a relief! I must transplant this dying heart, let it beat strong again, let a tree grow lush with swaying leaves.

비틀거리는 바다

한쪽으로 자꾸 기울어지는 걸음 왼쪽 머리의 통증 때문이었을까 아니면 오른쪽? 밤새 달달 끓여서 수증기로 날리려 용을 쓰던 달빛의 노력이 가상했지만 쓸데없는 체력소모인 줄은 알았지. 자꾸 떨어지는 머리의 무게 때문에 커다란 열기구 하나 달아야겠어. 아직도 내 영혼은 식물성인데 자꾸 냄새나는 동물성 먹이를 강요당해. 시시각각 비대해지는 몸뚱어리를 처연한 눈빛으로 쓰다듬네. 팽만한 배를 견디기 버겁거나 참을 수 없이 비위가 상할 때 변기를 거꾸로 끌어안고 토악질을 하곤 하지. 반쯤 녹아버린 동물의 뼈들, 못 감은 애꾸 눈, 팔딱이는 반쪽의 심장이 마구 쏟아져 나와. 재활용도 가능할 플라스틱 덩어리도 산만큼 게워냈네. 내 영혼은 아직 식물성! 식물성! 식물성 주문을 외워. 한도 초과한 몸뚱이의 주인이 아직도 나인 줄은, 두터운 비계층을 받치고 있는 질식 직전의 늑골을 만질 때야. 육신대는 사색의 푸른 갈비뼈! 아, 얼마나 다행인지! 죽어가는 심장을 서둘러 이식해야겠어. 다시 힘차게 뛸 수 있기를, 잎새 너울거리는 나무도 무성하게 자라날 수 있기를.

Becoming a Mourner

Hurrying to lay a flower path,
the tears of beheaded blooms
spill wide—
I don't even ask for fragrance,
but the taxidermied grief stands vivid.

Buried in flowers whiter than snow,
you dazzle today—
was any living day
ever this bright?

Between you and us,
an uncrossable river flows—
on this bank, people
button up solemnly,
place a flower,
burn incense,
dab powder to stage sorrow.

Those not so sad
share out grief,
one bite each.
〉

No set order—
when called,
it could be me or you next.
To mark this day,
to boldly prove I live,

I wrote my name
in the guestbook.

弔客이 되어

서둘러 꽃길을 놓느라
애꿎게 목 잘린
꽃들의 눈물이 질펀하다
향기까지야 바라지도 않지만
박제된 비통悲痛이 선명하다

백설보다 흰 꽃들에 쌓여
오늘 당신은 참 눈부시구나
살아있던 어떤 날이
이보다 더 빛났을까

당신과 우리 사이
건너지 못할 강물이 흐르고
이 켠 강기슭 사람들은
한껏 엄숙하게 옷깃을 여미며
한 송이 꽃을 올리고
혹은 향을 사르고
분첩을 두드려 슬픔을 연출한다

그다지 슬프지 않은 사람들이
골고루 슬픔을 한입씩 나눠 먹는다

정해지지 않은 순번

호명하는 대로 다음 차례는
나 또는 너일 수도 있는
이 자리를 기념하며
오늘, 호기롭게
살아있음을 증거 하려
방명록에 내 이름을 적고 왔다

The Scarecrow' s Dance

Busy in my own way,
acting often joyful,
sometimes crafting elegant words—
taking on grand spells,
"Why not!"—
I drape myself in bravado.

A madman's sword dance
I can't cross sober—
I'd be a gourd of moonshine
splashed dazzling
over flashing blades.

The world's too perfect,
brimming with trust—
enduring as a hollow thing
grew too hard.

At day's end,
steeped in fatigue,
a measure of sadness,
a day's worth of emptiness,
follows me to bed.

허재비의 춤

나름 바쁘게
자주 기쁜 것처럼
가끔 우아한 말 짓까지도
벅찬 주문을 받아들고
까짓것!
허세를 걸쳐 입는다

취하지 않고는 넘을 수 없는
망나니의 칼춤
번득이는 칼날 위로
눈부시게 뿌려지는
한 바가지 탁주라도 되고 싶었다

세상은 너무 잘났고
미쁨으로 넘쳤으니
헛것으로 버티는 남루를
견디기 어려웠다

피곤에 절어 돌아오는
하루의 끝은
늘 얼마큼의 슬픔
하루만큼의 허탈이
따라와 눕는다

Sometimes, Occasionally

Today,
I want to do nothing,
be nothing.

Peeling off
the name tags strung on me,
I'd become a tranquil scene—
eyes closed, swaying lightly,
carried by the wind.

가끔, 때때로

오늘은
아무것도 하기 싫다
아무것도 아니고 싶다

어쩌다 주렁주렁 매단
이름표 다 떼어놓고
적요로운 풍경이나 되어
눈감고 살랑살랑
바람에 업히고 싶다

Old Hope, I Want to Be a Lover

Wife, daughter-in-law, mother—
names I gained meeting you,
worn over half a century,
tattered and dry—
I'd strip them off.

A tender woman gazing with wet eyes,
heart thrilling
at a steady look—

Shedding the burden of service,
I, too, want to be his lover now.

老望, 애인이 되고 싶다

마누라 며느리 엄마
당신을 만나 새로 얻은 이름
반세기 넘게 써먹어서
너덜거리고 푸석한
그 이름 떼어내고

글썽이며 바라보는 애틋한 여자
지긋이 눈 맞추면
찌르르 가슴이 먼저 젖는 여자

섬김의 짐을 벗고
이제 나도 그의 애인이 되고 싶다

Time, That Trifle

At forty,
I dreamed of achieving something—
fumbling, I missed it,
and forty-nine felt sad.

Fifty came, then sixty,
fearlessly drifting to seventy-something—
an unstoppable current.

That trifling time,
neither sad nor not—
will I reach eighty unscathed?

Like clouds borne by wind,
I'll flow where time pushes,
drifting off
like the moon trails clouds.

세월 그까짓 것

마흔이 되면...
뭔가 이룰 것 같은 꿈이 있었지
어영부영 마흔을 놓치고
마흔아홉이 슬펐네

쉰이 되고 예순이 되고
겁도 없이 일흔몇까지
떠내려왔어
불가항력의 표류

셈법도 놓아버린 그깟 세월
슬프지도 않지만
무사히 여든은 되어질까

바람에 떠가는 구름인 양
세월이 미는 대로
나는 흐르리
구름에 달 가듯이
흘러서 가리

Dream Place

Waking at midnight,
why do I miss you
so fiercely?
A wretched dream
in early sleep, perhaps.

You left me,
fading far away,
or I parted from you
forever—

The dream where I sobbed
must have hurt so much.
Even in time's taxidermy,
tear stains soak through.

꿈자리

한밤중에 자다 깨어
왜 그대가 사무치게
보고 싶을까
초저녁 선잠에
몹쓸 꿈을 꾸었나보다

그대가 나를 두고
아득히 멀어졌거나
내가 그대 곁에서
영영 떠나왔거나

흐느껴 울던 꿈자리가
몹시도 아팠던 모양이다
박제된 시간 속에서조차
눈물자국 흥건하다